ON LINE

Native Americans

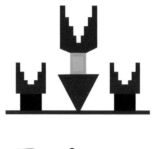

Paiute

Barbara A. Gray-Kanatiiosh

ABDO Publishing Company

visit us at
www.abdopublishing.com

Published by ABDO Publishing Company, 4940 Viking Drive, Edina, Minnesota 55435. Copyright © 2007 by Abdo Consulting Group, Inc. International copyrights reserved in all countries. No part of this book may be reproduced in any form without written permission from the publisher. The Checkerboard Library™ is a trademark and logo of ABDO Publishing Company.

Printed in the United States.

Cover Photo: Marilyn "Angel" Wynn/Nativestock.com
Interior Photos: Corbis pp. 4, 30; Index Stock p. 29; Mono Lake Committee p. 30; Nativestock.com p. 29
Illustrations: David Kanietakeron Fadden pp. 7, 9, 11, 13, 15, 17, 19, 21, 23, 25, 27
Editors: Rochelle Baltzer, Heidi M. Dahmes
Art Direction & Maps: Neil Klinepier

Library of Congress Cataloging-in-Publication Data

Gray-Kanatiiosh, Barbara A., 1963-
   Paiute / Barbara A. Gray-Kanatiiosh.
     p. cm. -- (Native Americans)
   Includes bibliographical references and index.
   ISBN-10 1-59197-657-X
   ISBN-13 978-1-59197-657-8
   1. Paiute Indians--History--Juvenile literature. 2. Paiute Indians--Social life and customs--Juvenile literature. I. Title. II. Native Americans (Edina, Minn.)

E99.P2G73 2006
979.004'9745769--dc22

2005049307

About the Author: Barbara A. Gray-Kanatiiosh, JD

Barbara Gray-Kanatiiosh, JD, Ph.D. ABD, is an Akwesasne Mohawk. She resides at the Mohawk Nation and is of the Wolf Clan. She has a Juris Doctorate from Arizona State University, where she was one of the first recipients of ASU's special certificate in Indian Law. Barbara's Ph.D. is in Justice Studies at ASU. She is currently working on her dissertation, which concerns the impacts of environmental injustice on indigenous culture. Barbara works hard to educate children about Native Americans through her writing and Web site, where children may ask questions and receive a written response about the Haudenosaunee culture. The Web site is: www.peace4turtleisland.org

About the Illustrator: David Kanietakeron Fadden

David Kanietakeron Fadden is a member of the Akwesasne Mohawk Wolf Clan. His work has appeared in publications such as *Akwesasne Notes*, *Indian Time*, and the *Northeast Indian Quarterly*. Examples of his work have also appeared in various publications of the Six Nations Indian Museum in Onchiota, NY. His work has also appeared in "How the West Was Lost: Always the Enemy," produced by Gannett Production, which appeared on the Discovery Channel. David's work has been exhibited in Albany, NY; the Lake Placid Center for the Arts; Centre Strathearn in Montreal, Quebec; North Country Community College in Saranac Lake, NY; Paul Smith's College in Paul Smiths, NY; and at the Unison Arts & Learning Center in New Paltz, NY.

Contents

Where They Lived

The Paiute (PEYE-yoot) language is from the Numic branch of the Uto-Aztecan language family. The name *Paiute* is thought to mean "water Ute." The Ute were neighbors of the Paiute. Other nearby tribes included the Bannock, Shoshone, Gosiute, and Navajo.

The Paiute were separated into two major groups. The Northern Paiute lived in parts of present-day Oregon, Idaho, Nevada, and California. The Southern Paiute lived in areas of modern Utah, Nevada, Arizona, and California.

Many different landforms covered Paiute territory. The southern areas contained deserts, where plants were scarce. In the north, there were grassy hills and open meadows. Mountains surrounded both areas.

Piñon pines continue to grow on Paiute homelands. Today, they decorate Capitol Reef National Park in Utah.

Paiute lands contained various types of plants. Spruce, juniper, and piñon trees were found throughout the territory. And, sagebrush grew in the plains and on the mountain slopes. There were also lakes, rivers, and streams on the land. Cattails, shrubs, and willows grew near these areas.

Paiute Homelands

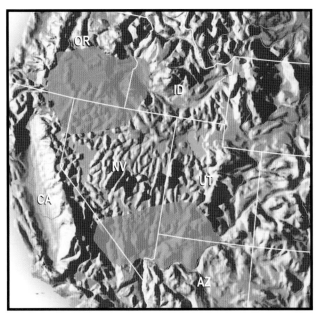

Society

The Paiute lived in settlements with **extended family** members. Usually three to ten families lived in each settlement. Sometimes groups of families formed bands. They named the bands after a nearby resource or geographic feature.

The Paiute were nomadic. So, the bands often separated to follow animal **migrations** and plant ripenings. Traveling was necessary for the tribe's survival.

At certain times of the year, the Paiute bands reunited. They fished together in the spring. In the autumn, they gathered piñon nuts and hunted rabbits and antelope. Prior to each event, the Paiute held a round dance. Performing this dance made the Paiute feel connected. It helped strengthen their society.

Each Paiute settlement had a headman, or leader. A headman was chosen because he was respected among the community. As a leader, he aimed to keep the people safe and happy. Before making an important decision, a headman made sure to hear from everyone in the settlement.

Medicine people called shamans were also respected members of Paiute society. Shamans used their supernatural powers to heal people, perform ceremonies, and bring good luck to hunters.

The Paiute held a round dance three times a year. At those times, tribe members danced in a clockwise circle around a center pole.

7

Food

The Paiute hunted, fished, gathered, and gardened. In the north, men hunted antelope, deer, elks, and mountain sheep. They used spears and bows and arrows to capture these animals.

Large animals were not always found in the southern areas. So, the Southern Paiute depended on smaller animals for food. The men hunted squirrels, rabbits, and gophers with traps and nets. They also caught rats, mice, lizards, and snakes.

The Paiute fished in the lakes and rivers. They used spears, nets, and traps to catch trout, suckers, and salmon. They often fished for salmon from willow platforms in the rivers. They also hunted ducks and geese near these waters.

At certain times of the year, animals were scarce. So, the Paiute depended on gathering plants for food. For this reason, the tribe held a deep respect for plants. As the women gathered, they prayed to the plant spirits. They collected fruits, cattails, camas bulbs, nuts, and seed. The women also gathered crickets, grasshoppers, and caterpillars.

The Paiute planted gardens in low areas that flooded when it rained. They depended on rain to sustain their crops. These foods included corn, beans, squashes, melons, and sunflowers.

Piñon nuts were an important food source for the Paiute. The women used poles to gather cones from piñon trees. Then, they roasted the cones and removed the nuts.

Homes

The Paiute lived in two types of homes. During the warmer months, they lived in temporary shelters called lean-tos. They lived in stronger homes called wickiups (WIH-kee-uhps) during the winter.

Lean-tos were easy to build while traveling. These simple shelters provided protection from light winds and rain. The Paiute used wooden poles and brush to make a frame. Then, they tied brush and cattail reeds to the frame to form the sides. Lean-tos had sloped, single-pitched roofs.

Wickiups provided more protection and warmth during the cooler months. Sometimes, the Paiute built a wickiup over a pit for extra warmth. First, they made a cone-shaped frame from willow poles. Then, they covered the poles with brush and cattail reed mats. Finally, the Paiute used willow or plant fibers to tie the frame and the mats together.

Inside the wickiup, there was a fire pit. The Paiute used fire to cook foods and to keep warm. Smoke escaped through a hole in the ceiling. The Paiute slept on beds made from woven cattail reed mats. To stay warm, they covered themselves with rabbit-fur blankets.

The Paiute lived in wickiups during the winter.

Clothing

The Paiute wore clothing made from plants and animals. The women often made the clothing using deer, elk, or antelope hides. First, they **tanned** the hides to make them soft enough to work with. Then, they sewed them together to make a piece of clothing. To do this, they used needles carved from bone and thread rolled from plant fibers or **sinew**.

Usually, the men wore **breechcloths** and shirts. And, the women wore dresses. But in the warmer areas, the Paiute did not wear much clothing. Sometimes the men wore only breechcloths.

During the winter and while traveling, both men and women wore leggings. These were made from sagebrush or bark. Also during the winter, the Paiute wore woven rabbit-fur robes. It took 40 rabbit hides to make just one robe!

To protect their feet, the Paiute wore moccasins or sandals. They made the moccasins from **tule** or animal hides. And, they wove yucca or bark to make their sandals.

The Paiute believe that life is sacred. So, they tried to use every part of a taken animal. Both men and women wore necklaces and earrings made from animal teeth, claws, or bones.

The Paiute painted their skin for several different reasons. Sometimes, they wore red body paint to protect their skin from the sun. Other times, they wore face and body paint for special dances or ceremonies. The tribe also **tattooed** their faces.

Paiute women's hats resembled the top of an acorn. Sometimes, men's hats were made from tanned hides and decorated with small feathers.

13

Crafts

Paiute hunters used duck decoys to attract birds. The decoys were fake birds that looked real when floating in the water. The tribe made these decoys from cattail reeds.

To form the pretend duck's head and neck, the Paiute used a bunch of fresh leaves. They wrapped twine around the bunch to hold it together. Then, they arranged more leaves to form the top of the head and the beak.

Next, the Paiute built the decoy's body from cattail stalks. First, they cut the stalks into 29-inch (74-cm) lengths. Then, they dampened the middle of each stalk to prevent breakage. Last, they wrapped the stalks around the bottom of the neck. This connected the head to the body.

Sometimes, hunters used real duck hides to cover the decoy. This made the decoy look even more realistic. Other times, the Paiute used leaves and stems as a cover. They wrapped fresh leaves around the front of the pretend duck. Then, they tied the stems of the leaves together at the back of the neck and near the end of the body. To form the tail, they cut the stem ends. The decoy was then ready to be placed into the water.

To catch ducks, Paiute hunters placed a decoy in the water. They waited near the decoy until a flock of ducks paddled close enough. Then, they threw a net over the ducks to capture them.

Family

In Paiute society, every family member helped with daily tasks. Duties depended on age and gender. And responsibilities changed with the seasons.

During the spring, the men fished while the women dug for roots. And in the summer, the women gathered seed and berries. When autumn came, the women gathered seed and nuts. In late autumn, the men came together to hunt rabbits and antelope. They chased rabbits into nets and antelope into brush **corrals**. Once they had the animals trapped, the men killed them for food.

There were some responsibilities that lasted all year. The women raised children, made clothing, and prepared food. They often mixed dried foods with water in a basket to make soup. To warm the soup, they placed hot stones inside the basket.

Paiute elders often stayed in the settlements while the younger people traveled. The elders tended the gardens. During the winter when everyone was together again, they told stories to their families.

A shaman oversaw antelope hunts. His powers were believed to lure the animals into corrals.

Children

Paiute children learned by watching and assisting the adults. Boys and girls helped with daily tasks, such as gathering nuts, berries, wild plants, and seed. They used seed beater baskets to knock seed from the grasses into larger carrying baskets. The children also uprooted cattail shoots and camas bulbs with digging sticks.

The women taught the girls how to weave coiled and twined baskets. To make a coiled basket, the girls wrapped strips of fibers, wood, leaves, or grass into a bundle. Then, they rolled the bundle into a spiral. They wove twined baskets from grass or strips of cedar bark and root fibers. Girls also learned how to weave twined sandals from cattail plants and corn husks.

Boys learned how to hunt and fish. The men also taught them how to make arrowheads, nets, and fish traps. They wove nets from rolled plant fibers. And, they built traps from willow twigs and **cordage**.

In their free time, children enjoyed playing games. And, elders often taught them about Paiute **culture** and history. Children also learned traditional songs and dances.

Paiute girls learned how to make coiled and twined baskets. They often made twined seed beater baskets.

Myths

The Paiute pass on stories about the Sky World. These myths tell of how the sky people left trails in the sky. These trails can still be seen today.

Long ago, a mountain sheep named Na-gah roamed Earth. He wore two large hoop-shaped earrings. Na-gah loved to climb. His father, Shinoh, was very proud of him. Shinoh smiled every time he saw Na-gah on top of a mountain.

Na-gah always looked for the tallest mountain to climb. And one day, he found it. But the mountain had steep, smooth sides with no clear path to follow. Na-gah felt disappointed. He was afraid he would disappoint his father if he couldn't reach the peak.

Then, Na-gah discovered a crack in the mountain. He ventured inside and found a tunnel. Na-gah traveled through the tunnel and finally saw light. He followed the light to an opening. As he stepped out, the opening disappeared. Na-gah found himself on top of the tallest mountain peak!

Shinoh saw Na-gah, but he realized the peak was too steep for Na-gah to climb down. Shinoh did not want his son to die, so he changed him into a star. He called him the North Star. To this day, the North Star is the brightest star in the sky.

Na-gah the mountain sheep was turned into a star. Today, he helps lost travelers find their way home.

21

War

The Paiute were usually peaceful people. They spent most of their time hunting and gathering food. However, sometimes war was necessary to protect their people and lands.

Prior to fighting, warriors asked shamans to protect them. Then, war leaders carefully planned out attacks. The Paiute knew their environment very well. Many times, they hid in cattail patches and then **ambushed** their enemies. Warriors used bows and arrows, spears, and wooden clubs during battle.

Eventually, Spanish explorers changed the way the Paiute fought. As the explorers traveled, they left behind horses. The horses soon populated much of North America. The Paiute began to use them during battle. The tribe split into fighting groups named after Paiute leaders. Then, they attacked settlers and travelers.

The Paiute participated in several wars against the new settlers. From 1858 to 1859, the Paiute fought in the Coeur d'Alene War. The Paiute War followed in 1860. And in 1878, they fought in the Bannock War. Each time, they battled to protect their people, land, and **culture**.

Horses helped the Paiute
travel faster and farther.
The tribe also used
them during battle.
The Northern Paiute
became especially
skilled riders.

Contact with Europeans

In 1776, a group of Spanish explorers ventured into Utah. There, they encountered several Paiute women gathering seed. These explorers were the first Europeans to make contact with the Paiute. Trappers, traders, and **emigrants** followed soon after.

In the late 1840s, the gold rush lured miners to Paiute territory. And after the discovery of silver in the 1850s, even more people settled there. In 1851, the first group of Mormon **missionaries** arrived in southern Utah.

The new settlers were different from the Paiute. They brought **domestic** animals, which had diseases that made wild animals sick. The settlers cut down many piñon trees to use for wood and fuel. And, they forced many Paiute to work for them.

The Europeans also brought sicknesses that the Paiute had no defenses against, such as smallpox. Many Paiute died from disease or starvation. Their population was quickly reduced. And, hope was starting to fade.

Around that time, the Paiute began to embrace the Ghost Dance religion. They believed that this religion would eliminate the new settlers and bring back their dead ancestors.

The Paiute believed that performing the Ghost Dance would restore their traditional lifestyle.

25

Wovoka

Wovoka (woh-VOH-kuh) was a Paiute leader. His name means "the cutter" in the Paiute language. He is also known as "Jack Wilson." Wovoka is thought to have been born in 1858. He grew up in Mason Valley, Nevada.

On January 1, 1889, there was a solar eclipse. At the same time, Wovoka became ill with a fever and had a spiritual vision. In his vision, Earth had returned to a natural state. Large animal herds roamed unfenced lands and there were no Europeans.

In the vision, Wovoka spoke with his dead ancestors and the Great Spirit. They told him that if the Paiute wanted a restored Earth, they should reject European ways. The Paiute were to pray, **meditate**, dance, and stop drinking alcohol. The Great Spirit also told Wovoka to do the round dance to bring peace. These ideas developed into the second movement of the Ghost Dance religion.

Wovoka is said to have had mystical powers. During a severe dry spell, he made ice flow in a river. Another time, he made ice fall from trees. And, he could not be harmed by gunpowder.

Soon, Wovoka's feats and his message of peace spread throughout America. When other Native Americans heard of these achievements, they traveled across the country to visit him. Wovoka died in 1932.

Wovoka founded the Ghost Dance religion. His father was a shaman and the assistant to Wodziwob. Wodziwob was the leader of the first Ghost Dance movement in 1869.

The Paiute Today

In 1926, a survey showed that most Native Americans were living in poverty. So in 1934, the U.S. Congress established the Indian Reorganization Act. This act aimed to promote self-government among the tribes by decreasing federal support and control. This worked well for many tribes. Some tribes adopted councils with **constitutional** governments.

However between 1954 and 1960, the U.S. government stopped aiding tribes that seemed able to support themselves. This included the Paiute. During this time, some tribes struggled to reorganize themselves without the government's support.

Unfortunately, some people took advantage of this situation. It was easier for them to claim tribal territory because it was no longer supervised by the government. The Paiute lost many acres of traditional hunting and gathering land. Native Americans protested, and in 1960 changes were made. Some tribes were paid for lost land.

Today, the Paiute have **reservations** in Oregon, Nevada, California, Utah, and Arizona. These include the Burns Paiute Reservation in Oregon, the Moapa River Reservation in Nevada, the Big Pine Reservation in California, the Kaibab Reservation in Arizona, and the Paiute of Utah Reservation. The Paiute share some reservations with other tribes. In 2000, there were about 13,500 Paiute.

Paiute-Shoshone petroglyphs were found in California. These carvings or inscriptions on a rock represent something. The exact meanings of petroglyphs are unknown.

A pair of traditional Paiute moccasins

This Paiute woman uses a cradleboard to hold her child. Cradleboards were commonly used among nomadic Native American tribes. When traveling, cradleboards served as a safe way to transport babies.

Paiute Lucy Tellis worked for four years to complete this basket. In 1933, Tellis was rated the champion basket maker of the Yosemite National Park District in California. This basket is larger than those produced today.

Glossary

ambush - a surprise attack from a hidden position.

breechcloth - a piece of hide or cloth, usually worn by men, that wraps between the legs and ties with a belt around the waist.

constitutional - of or relating to the laws that govern a country.

cordage - ropes or cords made by twisting plant fibers.

corral - a pen or an enclosure for capturing livestock.

culture - the customs, arts, and tools of a nation or people at a certain time.

domestic - of or relating to animals that are tame.

emigrate - to leave one's country and move to another. People who emigrate are called emigrants.

extended family - a family that includes grandparents, uncles, aunts, and cousins in addition to a mother, father, and children.

meditate - to be in a state of quiet, careful consideration and thinking.

migrate - to move from one place to another, often to find food.

missionary - a person who spreads a church's religion.

reservation - a piece of land set aside by the government for Native Americans to live on.

sinew - a band of tough fibers that joins a muscle to a bone.

tan - to make a hide into leather by soaking it in a special liquid.

tattoo - a permanent design made on the skin.

tule - a type of reed that grows in wetlands. Tule is native to California.

Web Sites

To learn more about the Paiute, visit ABDO Publishing Company on the World Wide Web at **www.abdopublishing.com**. Web sites about the Paiute are featured on our Book Links page. These links are routinely monitored and updated to provide the most current information available.

Index